The Success Code

The Success Code
Book II
More Authentic Power Principles for Creating Your Dream Life

By
Dr. Joe Rubino

Praise for The Success Code Books

This book is Dr. Joe's masterpiece! A brilliant system for reaching great heights. A road map to the principles of life that spell super-success for anyone who is willing to apply them. This book should be read — no, it should be devoured! — by everyone.

Bob Burg, Author,
Winning Without Intimidation

Dr. Joe Rubino's books are profoundly life-changing. The principles and experiences he outlines can cause transformational break-throughs in all aspects of life: business, per-sonal, family, financial and recreational. Dr. Joe's genius in communicating life experience and empowerment is manifested in an easy-to-apply format. It's a must for everyone wishing to be the best they can be.

Dr. Tom Ventullo
President, The Center for Personal Reinvention

An easy reading road map showing you how to succeed in today's world. Recommended.

Joe Vitale
Author, Life's Missing Instruction Manual

Even with knowledge, passion and purpose, success in any endeavor can be road-blocked by our own blind spots. The success principles in Dr. Joe Rubino's books unlock our greatest winning potential. If you're up for breakthrough success and a tool to unlock the answers within, here is your guide!

Connie Dugan
Director , The Heart of Business, Inc.

The Success Code books are "models of reader friendly accessibility as Rubino relates the keys to accessing personal power, including the skills of listening, creating a structure for maximizing effectiveness and fully connecting with others, eliminating daily upsets, honoring core values, ending gossip, developing personal charisma, and more. Very highly recommended additions to any personal or professional self-help, self-improvement, self-discovery studies program."

The Midwest Book Review

The Powerful Person

You are:
Committed to the question
And to not knowing the answer.
Committed to the result
Yet not attached to it.
Always open to possibilities
Recognizing when you are not.

Joseph S. Rubino

The price of greatness is responsibility.

Winston Churchill,
Prime Minister of the United Kingdom,
1940-1945 and 1951-1955.

The reasonable man adapts himself to the conditions that surround him...
The unreasonable man adapts surrounding conditions to himself.
All progress depends on the unreasonable man.

George Bernard Shaw,
Irish-born English dramatist,
critic, and essayist, 1856-1950.

The most basic choice we have in life is whether to bring our creative and expressive energies out into the world in positive or negative ways. No matter what our circumstances, we have the power to choose our directions.
In each of us are heroes, Speak to them and they will come forth. We have to live and we have to die; the rest we make up.

Author Unknown

Winning is a habit. Unfortunately, so is losing.

Vince Lombardi,
Green Bay Packers coach who led his team to 5
National Football League championships and 2
superbowl titles; known for his single-minded
determination to win.

The important thing is not to stop questioning.

Albert Einstein,
German-born American physicist
known for his theory of relativity.

All our dreams can come true — if we have the courage to pursue them

Walt Disney,
American cartoonist,
motion-picture producer and showman.

The Success Code, Book II: More Authentic Power Principles for Creating Your Dream Life

Vision Works Publishing

Copyright © 2007

By Dr. Joe Rubino

All rights reserved.

Published by Vision Works Publishing

(888) 821-3135 Fax: (630) 982-2134

VisionWorksBooks@Email.com

Manufactured in the United States of America.

ISBN 0-9728840-5-X

Library of Congress Number 2006929086

With this book YOU will:

- Discover the keys to unlock the door to success and happiness in life.
- Learn how your listening determines what you attract to you.
- Learn how to shift your listening to access your personal power.
- See how creating a clear intention can cause miracles to show up around you.
- Learn the secrets to making powerful requests to get what you want from others.
- Discover how to fully connect with others and champion them to realize their greatness.
- Learn to create interpretations that support your excellence and to avoid those that keep you small.
- Develop the power to speak and act out of your commitments.
- See how communication with others can eliminate unwanted conditions from your life.
- Discover the secret to being happy and to eliminating daily upsets.
- Learn how detaching from your emotions will support your happiness and personal effectiveness.
- Learn how to put an end to gossip and to stop giving away your power.
- Develop the ability to lead your life with direction and purpose, and discover what it's costing you not to do so.
- And more!!

The Success Code

Dedication

This book is dedicated to those possessing the courage to reinvent themselves daily out of a commitment to be their very best.

The Success Code

Contents

The Success Code

Acknowledgments

This book is dedicated to my coaches, Mike Smith of Bridgequest, Carol McCall of The World Institute Group and Richard Brooke of High Performance People.

Like its prequel, *The Success Code, Book I*, this book is a compilation of many foundational principles I acquired over the last 16 years working in partnership with these mentors and with the thousands of people I've coached, trained, and with whom I've worked in partnership.

Special thanks to my business partner and close friend, Dr. Tom Ventullo who shares my commitment to bring this work to the world through our two companies, Visionary International Partnerships and The Center For Personal Reinvention.

Thanks also to my wife, Janice, and my family for their unconditional love and support and for making this work and my commitment to others possible.

Special thanks go to the thousands of friends, course participants and visionary leaders who are committed to impacting others to lead lives of power and meaning.

And thanks to you, the reader, for your courage in taking on the life-long process of personal development. May you realize your commitment to make each new day better than the past one, always reinventing who you are to be the best that you can be.

I
INTRODUCTION

I. Introduction

First and foremost, I acknowledge your willingness to engage in the process of personal development. The fact that you are reading this book says that you are willing to enter into the realm of what you don't know you don't know. The principles that follow will cause you to inquire about who you are and how you might more fully access your personal power.

For those who have already explored the concepts presented in *The Success Code: 29 Principles for Achieving Maximum Abundance, Success, Charisma, and Personal Power in Your Life*, this book represents a continuation of the never-ending process. To follow are more questions and principles that lead to a better understanding of what it takes to maximize your personal effectiveness with others.

For those who have chosen this book to begin your personal exploration, to maximize your personal power and to become the best you can be, welcome to the inquiry.

As we discussed in *The Success Code, Book I*, the success principles that follow represent pieces to the puzzle asking, "Who are you being that either contributes to your power, charisma and effectiveness or detracts from it?"

Because these principles must be experienced to be acquired, take the time to explore the principles presented daily as you work, play and interact with your friends, family, associates and others. Remember that as information alone, they will show up as interesting and informative but will not fully impact your life and your relationships. Your willingness to grow and experience the insights that result from the personal development process will transform these distinctions from great ideas to useable tools contributing to your personal power and effectiveness.

The process of developing the principles to follow is analogous to learning to swim.

Although you could go to the library and read every book ever written on swimming, you would not be very effective at actually swimming until you immersed yourself in the water and developed the skills necessary to start swimming.

Information alone is not enough to acquire the foundational principles needed for optimum personal power. Likewise, experience alone is not necessarily the source of becoming effective in many areas of life including interpersonal relationships. If information or experience were "the answer," those with the most knowledge or experience would always be the most effective. We all know that this is often not the case.

The source of maximizing your personal power is neither knowing nor doing but being. And being cannot be taught or learned as information. For your effectiveness to be positively impacted, it is necessary to re-invent yourself consistent with a new image of the person you choose to be. This reinvention will be a function of the key principles you acquire.

As you take on the exercises to follow, keep in mind that there is no answer to decipher or destination to reach. Your effectiveness will come from researching what causes you to maximize your power personally and in your relationships. Instead of needing to find the answer, focus on the inquiry and insights will result. Declare yourself a novice in areas that may be unfamiliar, uncomfortable or outside of what you know. Take the pressure off and enjoy the exploration of new personal territory.

There is no such thing as failing - only experiencing. Your personal effectiveness and power will result from your willingness to be awkward and uncomfortable as you take on new and unfamiliar concepts. Do not get discouraged if the inquiry becomes uncomfortable or challenging. Your courage to break yourself up and re-invent who you are will result in your experiencing one breakthrough after another.

Lastly, allow yourself to enjoy the process. Personal expansion can be fun and exhilarating. The new success principles you acquire will bring you happiness, rich relationships and maximum personal effectiveness.

II

IMPACTING YOUR LIFE AND PERSONAL EFFECTIVENESS

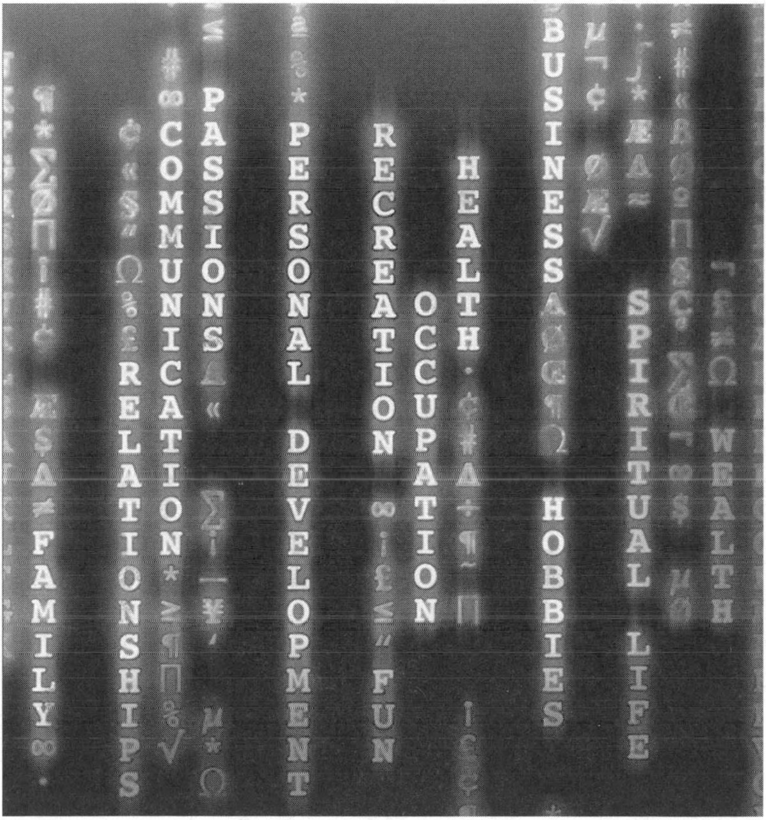

Creating a Structure for Getting the Most out of This Book

In order to get the most out of this work, you'll want to experience the concepts presented. One way is to hire some coaches and enter into a personal development program. Some recommended sources for these services are offered at the back of this book. After several years of experiencing the success principles daily, you'll notice that they will eventually become part of your being. Unfortunately, this is not always a practical approach for many people.

A good alternative is to get together with one to five other people who are committed to increasing their personal effectiveness. Request that everyone read through this entire book once first. Then commit to support each other to explore, digest, discuss and experience each concept one at a time, one each week.

As a group, create an alternating schedule for each person to take a turn leading the discussion around each key concept presented. Read each success principle together. Discuss any thoughts, insights, questions or challenges each one brings up for the group.

For the week that follows, immerse yourself in the principle presented, answering each of the questions offered at the end of each chapter.

Keep a daily journal (a spiral-bound notebook works well), recording any thoughts, observations, challenges, concerns or insights into the topic discussed. Look for revelations around increasing your personal power and effectiveness. Notice your interpretations or behaviors that do not support your excellence and relationships with others.

At the end of the week, get together with those in the group, in person or by telephone, and review what you learned. Discuss insights or breakthroughs you gained and rate your level of engagement on a scale from 1 to 10. Discuss any stops that may be limiting your participation or effectiveness.

Review those principles you've explored in

prior weeks as you take on each new concept. Do you see any patterns developing? Request feedback and insights from other members of the group. Although we can clearly see where others are stopped, we are the last to recognize our own limitations.

Once again, please have fun. Your willingness to laugh at yourself and enjoy the personal development experience will contribute greatly to your success.

III

PRINCIPLES FOR
ACCESSING YOUR
PERSONAL POWER

1

I am still determined to be cheerful and happy in whatever situation I may be, for I have also learned from experience that the greater part of our happiness or misery depends on our dispositions and not on our circumstances.

Martha Washington,
the very first U.S. First Lady

Coming to Terms
With What Runs Your Life

Early in life we make some important decisions about other people, the world and ourselves that have us seek out particular qualities while avoiding others.

At an early age between birth and about 12, we typically decide that we are not worthy of love, not good enough and somehow deficient in our makeup. We decide that we don't belong and create an explanation or justification for this because of what we think is wrong with us. If we could only get that thing we were lacking or become something we're not, we'd be all right. We'd belong.

We spend our lives avoiding this image we've created of what's wrong with us. We strive to become another opposite image we are driven to attain. By avoiding our past and living in the future, we fail to live fully in the present. There is thus no satisfaction possible in striving to attain an image that we never quite get to. It's analogous to climbing up the rungs of a ladder that extends into the clouds. The further up the ladder we climb in search of that image of ourselves, the more elusive it becomes. No matter how high we climb, it never is quite far enough for the ladder never ends. We are never quite good enough and never fully belong. This robs us of our happiness and power.

We spend our lives avoiding this inadequate image of ourselves but never have access to exactly what it is we are avoiding. Avoiding something only serves to keep it more firmly in place since we cannot create who we are in opposition to an image we are avoiding.

Ask yourself the following questions:

1) Who did you most admire and emulate when you were about 15 years old?

2) What did your parents most want you to be like?

Two of my heroes were Bobby Orr, arguably the greatest National Hockey League defenseman of all time, and Joe Namath, all-star quarterback legend for the New York Jets. Orr was the fastest skater on the ice in the entire game of hockey, the Boston Bruins' team leader and the good guy that made success happen. He was certainly a winner on and off the ice. Broadway Joe was strong and macho and had more women after him than he could handle.

My folks, like most parents, wanted me to be successful and responsible. They wanted the best for me and to be proud of me. I was driven to be all these things - cool, tough, macho, fast, smart and successful. With this image driving my actions, I went out for high school football and hockey hoping to live my life out of the picture I had created for myself.

At 5'5", 135 pounds and lacking the necessary skills, I never quite got there. I got trounced in football and lacked the speed, muscle and skill to be great in hockey.

So I decided to be smart instead. Being smart and clever was something I could be. So I became driven to be the smartest, most clever person I knew. I would study day and night seeking perfection. I would lie awake at night calculating how I would get ahead.

This resulted in the following accomplishments, but somehow they were never quite enough for me. Please pardon what may sound arrogant, as I believe it necessary to make a point.

• Valedictorian of my high school. (My 98 GPA was not good enough - I should have had 100.)

• Graduated in the top 4 percent of my class at Boston College. (Again that meant 80 out of 2200 did better than I did.)

• Graduated from dental school in three years, having finished my clinical requirements a full year ahead of almost everyone else. (No big deal. If I were really smart, I would have gone to medical school.)

Whatever I did was never enough, never satisfying for very long. After all, it never was winning the Stanley Cup in overtime by scoring the winning goal or winning the Super Bowl with a New York City tickertape parade thrown in my honor as everyone's hero.

As a dentist, I sought to have the biggest, most productive practice around. Every week presented the challenge of seeing more patients so as to beat the production numbers of the prior week. This need to be the biggest and best meant advertising to attract more patients and then hiring more dentists and staff to be able to accommodate them. But it was never enough. By the time I ended the lunacy - and the stress from the resulting overhead monster - I had a staff of 15 with six associate dentists all working to make our office the biggest and best around, attracting

250 or more new patients monthly.

All the while I was striving to become the images I held in my head - smart and successful - I was actually seeing myself as being weak, stupid, a failure. In other words, the high school kid who could never be Bobby Orr or Joe Namath. I still couldn't accept that I was not going to become cool, macho, tough and fast, so I kept running from the failure that I "knew" I "really" was. No matter what my most recent accomplishment was, I would find a way to make it insignificant, invalidating myself and making me once again that weak, stupid failure.

There was both no satisfaction in this setup and no peace. The more desperate my attempts to get to the nebulous image I pursued, the further I became from achieving it. So, what is the solution to exiting the vicious cycle?

First is the realization that your life is running out of control and is not your own. You are not running it. It's running you. Then become clear about what exactly it is that you are avoiding. When you can accept and become reconciled to what you are avoiding, you will stop being driven by it. When it becomes for you a big "so what!" the cycle will disengage and will lose its power to drive you.

Until it's perfectly all right for you to be seen by others as that very thing that you are determined not to be, it will use you and your life. Your job, relationships and life will be consistent with this drama.

The daily life upsets that you experience are about the threatening possibility that you'll become that which you are out to avoid at all costs. Any time the remote possibility shows up of you becoming what you fear, you will find yourself doing whatever it takes to avoid it. The image of being weak, stupid, a failure or whatever it is for you will come up and your immediate, often unconscious reaction will be, "NO, not that!" and you will seek to head off any possibility of it happening.

Now, being wired in this way does have its value. At times, it may serve you extremely well. After all, it's made you who and what you are today. However, as long as it runs you, you have no say in the matter. You cannot have a life of deliberate choice as you give your power away.

So, first get in touch with what images are running your life and dictating your actions. What qualities can you not stand other people to think characterize you as a person? Realize that you made this all up and it has become part of the drama that has run your life. It simply is not true and does not serve you any longer. If you shudder at the thought of being considered a weak, stupid failure, decide to embrace these qualities instead. Go out and create a bunch of failures and you will see that your successes will naturally come as a byproduct of your willingness to risk failure. Recognize moment by moment when the thought surfaces that you might become those dreaded qualities you fear and decide not to let these imagined thoughts influence your actions. This will provide you with the new and powerful freedom to act from the realization that you are able to deliberately choose your actions instead.

Reclaiming Your Power

1) Who did you most admire at age 15?

2) What qualities did your parents most want to see in you?

3) What images were or are you still out to become?

4) What or who are you out to avoid being? Notice when you are upset and in internal conflict. List those qualities you cannot tolerate and try to avoid at all costs.

5) Once you've identified what you are avoiding, notice when it is driving your behavior automatically.

6) Practice being in choice by recognizing when you are in your drama, controlled by your fears and act on purpose according to what best serves you at the time.

7) Record your observations daily in your journal.

If you do not change your direction, you are likely to end up where you are headed.

Chinese proverb

One of the best ways to persuade others is with your ears - by listening to them.

Dean Rusk,
U.S. Secretary of State in Pres. John F. Kennedy's
and Pres. Lyndon B. Johnson's cabinets

Listening Your Way to Greatness

What you listen for determines what you get from your conversations. Too often, we listen in a casual or unfocused way and come away with little. We often find ourselves listening to our own thoughts and internal chatter instead of to what the person is saying.

Let's examine a few ways you can get more by listening for more.

Listening for the Greatness in Others.

A characteristic that powerful people possess is the ability to empower others to be their best. This is the ability to see things in others that they do not yet see clearly in themselves while creating the space for them to recognize this potential and rise to the challenge. It's about seeing others as great without any attached demand that they live up to your expectations.

We instead typically listen from our opinions and judgments. Listening this way filters out what is actually said and distorts what we are able to hear. How we see others - as powerful or ineffective, intelligent or slow-witted, insightful or with little to contribute - has everything to do with what we get from conversations with them. When we hold others as great, we empower them to become so.

Getting the most out of others - our spouses, families, friends, co-workers, employees etc. - is made more likely if we consider them to have the potential to be greater than they see themselves.

By listening to people as though they already are magnificent, those positive qualities we expect to see in them readily show up. As we champion them to excel, they become aware of possibilities in themselves they did not previously see.

Listening to others routinely in this way enables them to gain confidence and strength until they see themselves as powerfully capable of producing whatever effect they desire.

The key to empowering others is to never offer the kind of help that makes them small, weak or dependent. Champion people by considering them already great and listen for the possibilities they represent. Support them to see what may be missing, that if put into place, would have them step into power.

Listen for what others need and want - not what you want. What you want is usually of little value compared to what they are ready to receive.

You have the gift to empower everyone who comes into your life. Likewise everyone has the same gift to contribute to you. Interact with others with the expectation that they have come to receive this gift of empowerment from you. Your job is to discover what that looks like. Through your listening to contribute to others, they give the greatest gift possible back to you. They have supported you to become the person you have chosen to be on purpose.

Listening for What Others Might Contribute to You:

If you enter into each conversation expecting to hear something of value you can utilize, you will likely come away with that very thing. While generating this listening is easy with someone you consider to be powerful or insightful, it will require returning yourself to your commitment to listen with a positive expectation when his or her speaking does not reflect this power.

For example, if you typically listen to others in an impatient way - hurry up and get to the point - you will need to remind yourself of your commitment to stay present in a conversation with a slow and deliberate speaker. Remember, someone's style of speaking may have little to do with what value you can garner from your conversation.

Listening for What Is Important to Others:

By putting yourself in the other person's world and developing an appreciation for his or her values and concerns, it is much easier to understand why they think, speak and act the way they do. Misunderstandings that might have resulted in confrontation or lack of affinity are replaced with an empathy that allows for exploration of common ground. When you can hear the commitments of others, you act with a compassion that results from your interest in what it's like for them to be who they are.

Listening with Something at Stake:

What we get from a conversation is often a function of what we have at stake. To illustrate this point, contrast how you typically listen to pre-flight safety instructions given by a flight attendant before take off. If you are like the rest of us, you're probably not really paying attention to what is said. You're probably either reading or distracted, figuring the chances of the plane crashing are slim to none. Besides, you've heard it all so many times before!

Compare this to a situation where, half way through the flight, the attendant announces that the engines have failed and the plane is going down. With your life at stake, you listen to the instructions like you have never listened before. Your listening is directly related to what you are listening for.

To gain the maximum amount from every conversation, listen from the viewpoint that everyone has something to share that is of great value. Your intent is to get it regardless of who the person is, how powerful you consider him to be and no matter what his style of speaking.

Listening for value in EVERY conversation will provide you with unending insights that you would not get from listening with less at stake.

Listening for the Good Intentions of Others:

Another valuable listening involves coming from the assumption that everyone operates from what they consider to be good intentions. I am NOT saying that this is necessarily true. It is simply an empowering interpretation to support you in your relationships. This can be particularly valuable when the evidence strongly suggests the contrary.

A controversial, extreme example is to consider that someone who we, in the western world hold to be as evil and deranged as Saddam Hussein, operates from what is to him the best of intentions. This is not to condone his horrible actions, and it ignores that his motivations have often been based in a drive for absolute power. It is merely to illustrate a point. When you step into another person's world and attempt to see things as they do, it is possible to imagine that they have acted from good intentions - in this case, for the betterment of his country.

Listening in this way allows you to come up with an alternative interpretation that supports the possibility of your relationship with the person. This perspective may support you at times and perhaps not at other times. It is entirely up to you to use this as just another tool in your toolbox to maximize your effectiveness with others.

Listening for the Greatness in Others

1) For the next 30 days, practice any or all of the following listening attitudes:

• To empower others to realize their greatness;

• To hear how they might contribute value to you;

• To appreciate their commitments and concerns and what it's like to be them;

• To listen with something significant at stake - perhaps your relationship to the other person; and

• To hear the good intentions of the other person.

2) In your journal, note any insights or possibilities that were created by listening to others in these ways.

3

Coming together is a beginning;
Keeping together is progress;
Working together is success.

Henry Ford,
American automobile designer and manufacturer

Bringing Out the Best in Others

One of the foundational principles that supports our power in relationships is our willingness to create room for the other person's stuff. By stuff I mean the way they view others, the world and themselves, especially when it is different from and in opposition to our perspective.

Everyone has their own unique combination of paradigms in which they view situations, circumstances and other people. When our paradigms match those of others, there's no conflict. That often characterizes a friendship where two people view life in much the same way. That's what friends often are for each other - righteous, matched opinions!

The challenge comes when others think and act in opposition to our perspective. Our usual reaction to such a conflict might be to oppose or distance ourselves from the other person.

This can be an opportunity to increase our personal power and effectiveness by listening with a commitment to the other person while standing in his shoes. Hold him as totally capable, intelligent and powerful and communicate from this empowering perspective. Don't be surprised if the person may actually listen to what you have to say!

When we disagree with others and hold them as stupid, mistaken, confused or just plain wrong, an impasse results and the relationship suffers. Making the other person wrong only prevents her from seeing things a different way. As the old saying goes, A man

convinced against his will is of the same opinion still.

Your willingness to give up your need to be
right and to dominate the other person is critical to empowering any conversation. As you
listen to the other person as someone totally
capable, competent and insightful, you now
have the ability to get them to see something
that they may not have been able to see
before. Make the other person great instead
of small - which is often what we do when we
don't agree with them.

Empowerment through listening will create the safety for the other person to try on a
different perspective and the space necessary
to convert to your point of view.

Connecting With Others

Too often we live in a state of isolation,
keeping others out to avoid losing our identi-
ty and to maintain control. Although we
crave intimacy, connectedness and love, we
disconnect if the threat of being over-

whelmed seems imminent. We might disconnect by creating an argument to ward off intimacy. We fight, grow apart and then need
love and acceptance. So we make up and get
back together again - for a while.

Becoming too busy to pay attention to the
other person causes a disconnection.
Worrying, becoming upset, leaving the room,
making the other person wrong, keeping lots
of other people around or listening to your
own thoughts instead of what the other person is saying are all ways to disconnect.

It is easy to opt for control, being right and
getting our way rather than finding a way to
enhance our relationships. To connect with
others, we must take our focus off of ourselves long enough to explore the possibilities
for mutuality. If we train ourselves to establish a mutual connection or means for relat-
ing, a synergy of purpose will result.

The best way to create mutuality is to
develop an appreciation for what it's like in
the other person's world. As you listen for the
other person's needs, wants, concerns, and

commitments, it is easier to develop the bond that comes from walking a mile in their shoes. By listening for commonality and how all parties might contribute something of value to each other, possibilities for enhanced relationships will evolve.

Bringing Out the Best in Others

1)   When you do not agree with family, friends and coworkers, do you empower them as you speak or do you make them small?

2)   In your daily journal for the next 30 days, record your reactions to and interactions with others with whom you do not agree. Rate each conversation from 1 to 10 - with 1 to signify that you're holding them as broken, stupid, wrong or deficient and 10 to mean totally capable, competent and worthy of all your respect and love.

3)   How does shifting your perspective impact your relationships?   How does it impact their openness to you?

Establishing Relatedness

1) In every conversation, develop an appreciation for what it's like to be that person. Listen for the other's concerns and commitments. How does this impact the relationship?

2) How does knowing their concerns and commitments affect your actions and provide a better appreciation for who they are and why they act as they do?

3) Listen for mutuality. What do you have in common that could further your relationship? How do your differences contribute to you both?

4) In what ways do you disconnect from others? Record in your journal each time that you do so.

There is no breakdown or breakthrough without a commitment. Successful people ask themselves, "Am I more committed to my goal or to whatever is getting in the way of achieving it?"

Carol McCall,
Founder of The World Institute's Listening
Course and expert on the art of listening

Listening for a Breakthrough

People have small, incremental levels of growth when their listening prevents them from having an insight or a breakthrough in their thinking. We typically listen to others from the perspective of whether we agree or disagree with what is being said. This limitation firmly roots us in our standard thinking process. When we listen to someone from the perspective of either agreeing or disagreeing, little can show up outside of this box.

If we agree with what is said, we probably knew it or it made sense to us already. If we disagree with what is said, we see it as having little value, so we discard it. In fact, we're probably already mentally preparing our arguments without listening any further to what they're saying. Listening from this perspective offers us little in fresh knowledge but great psychological rewards. It makes us right and we are addicted to being right.

The true value of listening effectively involves the intention of listening in an entirely new and different way-one in which we seek to discover something of value that we did not previously know. To generate such an empowered listening attitude, you must be willing to give up your need to be right and instead listen for new and expanded possibilities to appear. Recognizing when you are feeding your addiction to be right by agreeing or disagreeing and deliberately choosing to listen for new possibilities will result in discovering new uncharted terrain that you did not realize existed before.

Listening for a Breakthrough

1) Generate a listening for new possibilities in all of your conversations. Practice thinking outside of the box.

2) Catch yourself when you are listening to agree or disagree with others.

3) Record your observations in your journal daily.

5

Great minds have purposes, others have wishes.

Washington Irving,

American author

Honoring Your Commitments by Having an Intended Result

We notice those things we look for. If fully present to life, our heightened awareness will lead to an unending sequence of new discoveries. When it comes to developing expanded life skills, our conscious intent to place ourselves in the developmental soup pot - while we turn up the heat - will result in countless daily opportunities that were previously invisible to us.

This process heightens our awareness of relationships and how easily they can be impacted, resulting in abundant insights into how we can improve the quality of life for all. Your commitment to the process as opposed to merely wishing for it to happen will make the difference.

There is no connection between what we want and what we get in life. Look around you and notice how many people want things. Ask an audience of 10,000 people if they want to be wealthy, and you'll get a pretty unanimous response. Although they might want wealth, most will never attain it. The world does not care what we want.

There is, however, a connection between what we get and what we are committed to experiencing. Commitment is that do-whatever-it-takes quality that keeps our eye on the prize. With commitment there is no turning back. Commitment will open up new possibilities that would not reveal themselves to someone with less at stake.

Compare this to how most approach a new endeavor: They are willing to do it as long as it's convenient. The trouble with such an orientation to convenience over commitment becomes apparent when problems arise. With the inevitable appearance of problems, the path of least resistance is to follow one's feelings and do what appears to be most convenient. This usually means quitting. It explains why most do not get what they want but instead get what they are committed to - their comfort. To break out of this self-sabotaging pattern, simply return to and remain present to your commitment as life forces you to choose between commitment and feelings.

Success requires clarity around what's at stake and what it is that you are committed to doing. Then, whether you feel like it or not, do it anyway.

As you develop the habit of honoring commitments, life will take on new direction. Deliberate, focused action toward goals will replace sitting around hoping that your wishes will come true. Successful people are those willing to do what unsuccessful people are not.

Begin on the path of honoring your commitments and decide to live deliberately. Each moment ask yourself, "What is my intended result for this issue?" A clear intent will minimize the distraction and losing your way.

Exercising Your Commitment Muscles

1) List at least one deliberate goal you are willing to commit to achieving in the following areas:
- Your relationships
- Your health
- Your finances
- Your career

2) What definitive action steps will you commit to in order to achieve them?

3) In your journal each morning, record what your intended results are for the day in each of the above areas. What action will you take to bring you closer to your goal in each area?

6

The difficult truth to learn is that true change takes place in the imagination - in the images we hold.

Thomas Moore,
19th-century Irish poet,
satirist, composer and musician

Steps to Persuasively Influencing Others

The following sequence can be utilized to guide a conversation with persuasion and influence. Adhering to these principles creates an opening to be heard and produces a bond through relationship development. This results in the action progressing for everyone's mutual benefit.

Whether conducting a successful sales presentation, creating the foundation for a solid business relationship, or enhancing overall communication, the principles still apply just to a greater or lesser degree.

First, create an opening to be heard by developing rapport and establishing trust and mutuality.

Rapport results from speaking authentically about areas of interest to the other person. These might include topics such as family, occupation, hobbies, passions or where they live. Getting to know the person and discovering with sincerity what it is like in his or her world is the first step to understanding their needs and wants. Only then will you be able to listen and contribute something of value. You might open up this conversation by saying something like, "Tell me a little bit about yourself."

Once you understand something about what the other person's life is like and what he or she values, you can then establish mutuality or what you have in common that would support all parties. Establishing rapport and creating an opening to explore mutual benefit is the first step toward creating trust. The foundation of trust creates an opening to be heard and sets the stage to take the conversation to the next level.

Next, get permission to find out what is important to them or missing in their life. Asking permission to explore possibilities will turn what might have been perceived as an invasion of privacy into a welcomed mutual conversation for possibilities. You cannot possibly know how you might influence someone if you are unaware of what they consider valuable.

Let them know the reason for your request is to get to know them better. For a sales presentation, it might be to look with them to see if there is a fit for what you have to offer. If you are meeting a new potential business associate, it could be to explore if your company represents an opportunity the person is seeking. If you are speaking with a new acquaintance, it might be to explore common interests you share. Letting people know the source of your request to know them better will put them at ease and allow them to hear your commitment to them.

Speak your commitment to them in some way.

For an opening to influence another, let them know you share a commitment to supporting them. At the very least, share your interest in exploring the process to see if together you might uncover some mutual benefit. You might state your commitment as, "My intention is to look with you to see if there might be some mutual interest or benefit that could come from exploring possibilities with you. My commitment is to support your efforts in any way I can."

Create rich possibilities that inspire action.

People will enroll in your offer if you create value for them to want to look further. If

they are not interested in exploring potential-
ities with you, take the perspective that you
have not created possibilities that are rich
enough. Take this interpretation, not necessarily because it is true, but because it
empowers you to take full responsibility for
the result you wish to accomplish.

*Make a request that moves the action for-
ward.*

Before you make a powerful request, you
will have learned enough about the person to
get a sense of what is important to him. You
will have created an appreciation for what
you have to say out of your mutual interests.
Your request will bring you both closer to the
intended result. Because your conversation
has created the foundation for your request
to be heard, you have a much better chance
of influencing the person to be persuaded to
comply with your request.

Your dealings have been integrity based
and focused on leaving others whole. Out of
the respectful energy you have created, the

person is empowered to want to look with you in partnership to see what might be possible. You have influenced with integrity and possess the personal power to persuade others to want to accommodate you if possible.

Persuasively Influencing Others

1) Practice influencing others by following the sequence suggested. Describe your plan in your journal.

2) Record any insights afterward in your journal.

7

Thunder is good, thunder is impressive; but it is lightening that does the work.

Samuel Clemens,

also known as Mark Twain,

American author and humorist

Making Powerful Requests

The best way to access your power is by making requests that move people into action. By moving the action forward, you take an insight into what would support somcone and make a request that moves the person to accomplish something that would otherwise never be realized.

Most pcople operate out of a mistakcn notion that information is the source for action. Information alone, without action to move a situation forward, produces no results. A request is a conversation that produces action. So, if requests move people and situations forward, why don't we make them more routinely to generate results?

1. We may be fearful of having our requests declined. With the mere possibility of getting turned down, we will retreat and hide under a rock. A good example is asking out a date. You might really want to date that special person, but that little nagging voice reminding you that you just might get turned down can cause paralysis. If you are more committed to getting the date than protecting yourself from potential rejection, you'll pop the question. If the reverse is true, you might never know if the answer would have been ...YES!

2. We are more committed to looking good (and not looking bad) than to making a difference by making a powerful request. When your focus is on yourself, you trade in your ability to influence others for protection and comfort.

3. We are not clear about what requests to make and what needs to happen to bring about a result. So rather than determine what requests need to be made to produce an intended outcome, we do nothing and hope for the best.

4. We are not skilled at making requests so they can be heard and acted upon. When our requests are selfishly motivated or not in the best interest of the other person, they fall on deaf ears.

One way to get our requests heard and acted upon is to combine our request with a promise. I request that you do (whatever), and if you do, I promise to do (this) in return. Having your requests accepted and acted upon will depend on how effective you are at creating an opening for what you have to say. Create a receptive audience for your requests by speaking your commitment to the person or situation so that the reason behind the request can be appreciated. Example: Out of

my commitment to support you to be powerful, I request that you make at least three
requests every day whenever you see an
opportunity to influence a situation.

For effective requests, be clear about what
must be accomplished to satisfy the request
and by when you request it be done. Example:
I request that you hire a personal development coach by the first day of next month.

Whenever a request is made, the person to
whom it is made has four options: to accept
the request; to decline the request; to commit
to respond to the request by either accepting
or declining by some later date; and to propose an alternate possibility.

Should you opt to decline a request made
of you, leave the person making the request
whole. When possible, propose a counter
offer to benefit all involved.

Exercise for Making Powerful Requests

1) Make a request to move the action forward at least three times daily. Create a receptive audience for your requests to be heard and include a deadline with each one you make.

2) Record the results of your requests in your journal.

8

If you would win a man to your cause, first convince him that you are his sincere friend.

Abraham Lincoln,
16th U.S. President

Championing Others

As you more fully realize your personal power, you'll become increasingly aware of your ability to influence others. Knowing you can affect change will alert you to daily opportunities to make your contribution to the world.

One way to impact others is to champion them to notice and step into possibilities that they previously had not seen. Bring out the best in others by stretching them to be better each day. One way to do so is by acknowledging people. By acknowledging some noble quality you perceive in them, you allow them to step into a possibility you have created for them. You might speak your acknowledgment as a declaration you make for them. For example, you might say, "I acknowledge you for the courage you display in doing whatever it takes to grow personally and take the focus off of yourself. I see great possibilities for you to impact others."

Through acknowledgment, you recognize a worthwhile quality you perceive and offer it as a possibility to take on to support them to expand who they are. Instead of highlighting what does not work, focus instead on what they already have that you would like to see more of in them. Speak the possibility you see for them to create an image they can adopt as their own. You will thus have inspired them to take one step closer to realizing their excellence.

Exercise Your Ability to Champion People to Achieve Their Greatness

1) Look for positive qualities to acknowledge and reinforce in others.

2) Daily, acknowledge at least three people for qualities that would contribute to their excellence and inspire them to develop these traits.

3) Record your observations and insights in your journal.

9

Growth in wisdom may be exactly measured by decrease in bitterness.

Friedrich Nietzsche,
German philosopher, poet and critic

Creating Interpretations That Support Your Excellence

It is not possible for us to be totally effective with people and powerful in addressing daily situations if we are incomplete with our past. Any past relationship or experience that continues to require our attention and consume our energy prevents us from focusing on present-day happenings. These incompletions that we carry with us from our past are the source of many of our daily conflicts. They run our lives and prevent us from being open to maximizing new possibilities.

Living in the past fuels the misinterpretation machine we are inclined to frequent as part of the human condition. We tend to confuse what actually occurred in a given situation with the interpretations we make up, or create internally, about it. Our failure to distinguish what happened from what we made up causes us to operate from incorrect assumptions. This context then serves as a filter through which we view the world from that point onward. Every experience we encounter from our filtered perspective further strengthens the filter, reinforcing the interpretations we made up in the first place.

Notice the following example. Every day, two friends, Jim and Bob, pass each other on the street as they walk in opposite directions to work. Each day, Jim waves, "Hi, Bob," and Bob responds, "Hello, Jim." Day after day, Jim and Bob greet each other in this fashion.

One day, as they pass, Bob waves, "Hi, Jim." Instead of responding in kind, Jim looks down and keeps on walking. Seeing this, Bob thinks, "My wife Betty was right. Jim is jealous of our new house. After all these years, you would think he'd be happy for us. Well, who needs him anyway? I'll show him!"

The next day, as they approach, Bob decides to cross the street to avoid being snubbed by Jim. Jim notices Bob avoiding him and thinks, "What a snob. After all the years we've known each other, he decides to treat me like this. I'll show him!"

The next day as the two former friends draw near, both turn their heads and ignore the other. It is now perfectly clear to each of them that the other guy is a jerk and definitely has a problem.

Based on this certainty, from this day forward Bob and Jim not only ignore each other but avoid all contact with their families at every social situation. As this continues, the ill feelings between the two families grow until each has shared their side of the story with their friends, further escalating the conflict.

Going back to that first day when Bob waved and Jim didn't respond, Bob didn't realize that Jim had just come from an argument with his wife. Leaving the house, he was totally preoccupied. While Bob assumed that Jim ignored him purposely because of jealousy, what he took to be a fact was merely his interpretation of the situation based on something that was said in the past. Bob now sees the world from this new and distorted reality.

His actions were in line with the interpretation he saw as the truth. His action elicited a reaction consistent with this new behavior. On and on went the downward spiral of their relationship.

Too often, we confuse the facts with some negative or disempowering interpretation we make up. We then act consistent with this interpretation we now hold as true.

Because our interpretations are always made up anyway, why not make up something that supports you and others to be empowered in your relationships?

You always have a choice. Ask yourself, "What are the facts around what actually happened?" Then, "What is an empowering interpretation that I can make up about these facts that will support life working?" Notice that your empowering interpretation never has a mood of anger, fear or sadness attached to it.

This is one thing that is never handled. The moment you forget to be responsible for separating facts from interpretations, you are back in the soup! It is always juicier to create an interpretation that makes you right, better than someone, allows you to avoid responsibility or lands you in your familiar mood of anger, fear or sadness.

For life to work and your relationships to be strengthened, rigorously manage your interpretations. Mastering this principle can dramatically alter the quality of your life. You have the power at any moment to transform who you have been into the person you choose to become simply by managing your interpretations rigorously.

Creating Interpretations
That Do Not Support You

Now that we have examined how to create empowering interpretations, let's look further at why anyone might choose interpretations that do not support happiness and relationships. We touched upon the rewards we get from creating interpretations that put us in our addicting mood of anger, sadness or fear. They make us right and make the other person wrong. They allow us to dominate others and avoid being dominated. They allow us to justify ordinarily unjustifiable behavior. We get to avoid being responsible for our actions and our relationships with others.

Because these rewards are so addictive by nature, the lure of creating interpretations that allow us to be better than others is extremely strong. Only by realizing what these self-defeating interpretations are costing us can we fully appreciate the downside.

The biggest cost to being right and dominating others is relationships. We sacrifice love and intimacy with those closest to us and affinity and partnership with all others when we choose to dominate instead. By avoiding responsibility for our relationships, our health, well-being and vitality suffer. We trade our happiness and self-expression for the short-term fix of accessing our mood. Ultimately, creating interpretations that put us above others will cost us our life and life purpose.

Managing our moods takes noticing when we are in our predominant mood of anger, sadness or fear arising from negative interpretations. Then, separate what happened (the facts) from the mood-generating interpretation. Decide instead to choose a different, mood-free interpretation that supports you in your relationships.

Empowering Your Life by Shifting to Interpretations That Serve You

1) In every situation with the potential to produce an upset, ask yourself the following questions:

- What happened?
- What are the facts?
- What did you make up about the facts?
- What interpretations do not support harmony in your relationships?
- What more empowering interpretations will you make up to move life forward?

Record your observations in your journal.

2) What is your predominant mood? (It's usually some version of anger, sadness or fear.) Notice each time you are in your mood and record the circumstances in your journal.

3) In what areas of your life are you insisting on being right about something?

4) What is it costing you in terms of your health, dreams and relationships?

5) On a scale from 1 to 10, with 10 being

the most committed, how committed are you to giving up your need to be right in order to make your life work?

6) Record your insights in your journal.

10

It is the mind that maketh good or ill, that maketh wretch or happy, rich or poor.

Edmund Spenser, Renaissance English poet.

Detaching from Your Emotions

For the vast majority of people, each day presents another opportunity to ride the emotional rollercoaster. When things go our way, we are happy. When they don't, we react with anger, sadness, fear, disappointment, frustration, resignation, or any variation of hundreds of other emotional responses. In fact, we are typically so accustomed to experiencing these emotions that we take for granted that our lives will always be marked by emotional reactions to the challenges that life throws our way. We mistakenly believe that this is "normal" and everyone does it.

This belief that we are emotional beings reacting to situations and circumstances beyond our control that are not to our liking is so ingrained in us that we usually do not even see the possibility of living without these immediate varied emotional responses to situations. How many times have you heard people speak their belief that "We're human beings and we're entitled to our emotions?" These emotions are indeed juicy!

By coming from the perspective that we will always be at the effect of things that others say and do, thus provoking our emotional responses to these situations, we forfeit our ability to retain control of our emotional well-being. Our spouses say something that irritates us and we lash back. Our bosses criticize our work performance and we fear losing our jobs. We are left off the guest list for a neighborhood party and we react with sadness. We are unjustly accused of something we did not do, and we respond with indignant rage. You get the point. Life is full of opportunities to react in an emotional way that does not support our happiness, sense of peace, and our personal power.

So if our knee-jerk emotional responses do not support our happiness, peace of mind, or personal effectiveness, why do we continue to react automatically to the least little stimuli? If we hate being in such a state of constant low grade anger, why do we continue to find reasons to revert back to this state or to seemingly relish the opportunity to take our ever-present chronic state of low grade anger to a higher, more acute level? In the same way, we hate feeling sad but somehow, we find no shortage of opportunities that "make us" sad. Consider the person who is petrified of horror movies. The spooky scenes, bloody violence, and killings leave him agitated, feeling uncomfortable, and unable to sleep. But despite an aversion to these emotional responses, the horror movie addict continues to seek out the next, scarier, more gruesome movie that is guaranteed to stir up these same unpleasant emotions!

Clearly, we are emotional addicts. Although we may protest that we do not like feeling scared to death, down in the dumps (maybe even despondent), or filled with rage or vengeance, we seem to be at the mercy of these feelings. After all, we might argue, it's usually not our fault. The other guy is usually provoking us and we just react to these provocations with righteous indignation. The blame is over there, rarely with us. We are the victims and to blame us for such natural reactions is unfair! Even such an accusation would likely make most of us angry!

However, when we explore the nature of our emotional responses more closely, we may uncover some very interesting findings. Although we protest that we dislike feeling this way, our emotions make us feel alive. Within the anger we muster is a sense of personal power. Our angry response to a situation may allow us to regain control over some aspect of the situation. Perhaps, through our anger, we get to dominate the other guy who is likely out to dominate us as well. Perhaps our sadness provides us with a measure of consolation. We might feel sorry for ourselves and bask in the "poor me" sensations earned by most victims. Or perhaps our fear may prevent us from acting boldly and risking in some manner. By keeping us afraid and defensive, we stay safe. We may not have to deal with uncomfortable situations or the possibility of failing if we stay home and hide under the bed rather than face our fear in the cold, cruel world!

Although we may have become conditioned to feel that our emotional reactions are totally normal, (after all isn't everyone else reacting emotionally all around us?), we have the option of training ourselves to look deeper within when we feel the emotional warning - whether it be the adrenaline rush of anger as we get red in the face or the hollow sinking sensation of sadness in the pit of our stomachs.

Perhaps we might explore the true reason for our emotional reactions. Is there some label we fear or way of being that we are determined not to be associated with causing us to take the offensive? Is our anger truly at the person we lash out at or could our response be an attempt to conceal our own fears? Are we reading the situation in a manner that drives our emotional reaction? Might there be a better way to interpret what was said or done so that the emotional charge was absent? Could we give the other guy the benefit of the doubt or assume that his intentions were honorable? At the very least, could we assume that she is doing the best she can do considering her background experiences and how she has become accustomed to viewing the world?

When we are in personal development, we might take each opportunity that an emotional trigger offers us to stop for a moment and analyze the situation. What lies beneath that feeling of vengeance? What is the true source of the sadness we are feeling? How might we be avoiding responsibility for our part in the current state of affairs?

Rather than reacting with emotion to the circumstances, might we instead look upon the event as an opportunity to better understand why we are prone to act as we do? Might we instead welcome the chance to look at the situation without our typical attachment to an outcome or to being right? If we put ourselves in the other person's world, how might our perspective change? How would this shift in how we see things influence our emotional response?

Emotional awareness is the first step in changing your world and supporting others to transform theirs. It takes two people to dance. Once one changes her step, it is much more difficult for her partner to continue with the same dance he was previously doing.

The questions I have for you today are these:

• Are you willing to give up your right to react emotionally?

• Are you willing to allow your emotional cues to be your signal to explore what lies beneath your typical and customary reaction?

• Are you willing to detach from each emotional situation and look for the insights that await your discovery?

I can promise you that if you do, your life will never be the same!

Detaching from Your Emotions

1) In your daily journal, make note of each emotional reaction that occurs without your complete conscious awareness.

2) What types of emotions are usually present when you catch yourself in a knee-jerk type reaction?

3) What contrary benefits do these typical emotional responses provide for you?

4) How does creating a different interpretation about what happened support you in better managing your response to the situation and acting without emotion?

5) What insights have you gleaned about yourself as a result of detaching?

11

There's always a way - if you're committed.

Anthony Robbins,
American personal development
speaker, coach and author.

Making Promises and Keeping Your Commitments

In our culture, when we make a promise or commitment, we feel effectively locked into an obligation. With a promise comes a moral interpretation. What if I don't keep my promise? What will others think? How will I look? It becomes a trap or a should-do compulsion whether it still supports us or not.

As a result of this orientation to making a promise, we are reluctant to commit ourselves. Promises are seen as constraints. If I don't keep my promise, I will be seen as bad, as a liar. Seen in this light, promises provide us with no room to make powerful commitments. No one wants to volunteer to be bound against his will if his situation changes. A promise has no power if we are unable to revoke our promise responsibly if the commitment we made no longer supports us.

Take the interpretation that commitments can be made to empower you to attain some accomplishment just as an Olympic athlete commits to play full out for the gold medal. Whether or not she actually achieves the award does not diminish the value of the promise in propelling her into action. If a promise does not empower you to action, it probably is not worth very much.

When you've made a commitment and it no longer supports you, acknowledge what is so for you now and what has changed. Look for what can be put into place to make it work for all involved. Take responsibility for any consequences of revoking your prior promise. Tell the truth about what you are now willing to be responsible for and act accordingly.

Remember that life works to the degree that people keep their agreements. I am not advocating a careless or irresponsible approach to making promises. To make commitments you have no intention of honoring will not support you in your relationships with others.

Making Promises

1) Examine your relationship to making commitments. Where have you made a promise that now shows up like a have-to-do obligation that no longer supports you?

2) What can you do to responsibly acknowledge a change from what you were previously committed to doing?

3) What must you do to take care of any consequences to your change in commitment?

4) What new promises can you make to empower you with the freedom to act?

————12————

For every disciplined effort there is multiple reward.

Jim Rohn,
American personal development
trainer, author and speaker

Having the Courage to Act Out of Your Commitments

One of the biggest challenges that causes people to fail in achieving their goals and dreams is a tendency to act out of what is convenient in the moment. Acting in this manner puts you at the mercy of your present circumstances rather than making you the source of who you are and what you do. The decision to be the source of your excellence means deciding to trust yourself in the moment of decision to do the right thing. You commit to act from your principles rather than what might be most convenient at the time. This requires a ruthless commitment to honesty with yourself and others. You decide which is more important - your integrity or the temporary emotional conditions that result from taking the easy way out.

Mike Smith terms this critical moment of decision, The Y of Leadership.

Doing what is convenient	Contributing to others
Taking the easy way out	Doing the right thing
Doing what you feel like	Honoring your commitments
Looking good	Telling the truth
Being liked or popular	Risking
Selling others out	Acting for the benefit of others
Playing it safe	
Avoiding conflict	Making a difference

X You Are Here

Which Path Will You Take?

The decision to take the right path is one you will be required to make each time a new situation arises. You will need to choose between doing what feels good and is easier or safer or honoring your decision to personally expand who you are by risking, taking the focus off of yourself and acting from your commitments and the benefit of others. Your success will be related to generating courage in the moment of decision. This is never permanently handled, but must be chosen anew each time another opportunity presents itself.

As you decide time and again to act from your commitments, your self-trust will increase. When you make a mistake, forgive yourself and recommit to do better the next time. Your personal power will result from your courageous and never-ending declaration to act from the perspective of your commitments.

Exercise Your Commitments
to Yourself and Others

1) In each moment of decision, become aware of your option to choose to honor your commitments and values rather than what is most convenient at the time.

2) In your journal, record your progress in honoring your commitments instead of taking the easy way out.

13

'Tis a great confidence in a friend to tell him your faults; greater to tell him his.

Benjamin Franklin,
American statesman, author and scientist

He who fears he will suffer, already suffers because of his fear.

Montaigne,
16th-century French essayist

Complain to one who can help you.

Yugoslav proverb

Eliminating Unwanted Conditions

The life conditions you run away from always seem to follow you around! You attract those very conditions you seek to avoid because, by resisting them, you focus your attention all the more upon them. The act of wanting something actually pushes it farther away from you. The more you want something, the more you focus on the wanting of it and the fact that you do not have it, the more lacking it will be. Wanting is a declaration of lacking.

Diets are one such phenomenon. They are about resisting and suffering, and what we resist, we keep in place. Diets don't work long term because dieters see themselves as overweight. Rather than taking responsibility for having a toned, sleek and in-shape body, the dieter engages in a never-ending battle resisting being fat. To become that attractive, fit and energetic person, we must develop the habit of visualizing ourselves that way until we realize our expectation.

Being controlled by a partner is another condition often resisted. The more one spouse hates being controlled and opposes it, the more prevalent the condition becomes. If being controlled upsets you, you spend much of your time avoiding it. As a result, your focus is on the very thing you seek to avoid:

being controlled. Ironically, when you give up the right to control, you are back in control and the feeling disappears.

The same can be said about wanting to fix another person's upset condition. If we cannot stand to see someone stuck in a state of upset, we are likely to reinforce the upset. That which we resist will persist. Carol McCall reminds us that a person's upset with you is typically 99 percent about them and only 1 percent actually about you. Allowing people the space to be in their mood will provide them the freedom to let it go.

In a relationship where a partner demands more attention and affection than the other is prepared to give, this same dynamic is created. The more attention is demanded, the less likely it is to be given. If the freedom for either partner to leave the relationship does not exist, the freedom to stay likewise is missing. Because of obligation, resignation or habit, if a couple stays together without the freedom to choose, they will not likely find

contentment. If much of the reluctant partner's time is spent considering what it would
be like to leave, she lacks the freedom to con-
centrate on staying.

Being in choice about anything is the key
to succeeding at it. You cannot have a condition without allowing room for its opposite
condition. You cannot love someone if you
have no room to hate them. All life is a
dichotomy. The freedom to accept a condition, emotion or situation that we thought we
could not bear will create the room for the
unwanted condition to eventually disappear.

To the extent that you resist who you are,
you will be stuck with the condition you wish
to eliminate. So, stop resisting. Stop being
attached to a result. Commit instead to those
actions you can positively impact while giving
up your right to force your will or to demand
a result. You can still commit yourself to a
result without being attached to having it
happen. Fall in love with the person you are
and commit to managing the traits that do
not support you moment by moment.

We all have certain conditions we complain about. We say that these conditions are unwanted, but somehow, consciously or unconsciously, we keep them in place. We keep them around because doing so provides us with some reward. Keeping an unwanted condition in place allows you to justify or explain something or to not be responsible for taking action that would resolve the condition you say you do not want.

The key to having an unwanted condition disappear is simply your willingness to be rid of it. Decide to tell the truth about it. If you are willing to take responsibility for eliminating it, you will find a way to do so.

Ending Persistent
or Unwanted Conditions

1) In the areas of your health, relationships, career and finances, name at least one unwanted condition that persists in your life.

2) What are you resisting? How are you not being responsible for eliminating this condition?

3) What does keeping the condition in place allow you to justify or explain?

4) What specific dated actions will you take to effectively address and resolve this persistent condition? Or tell the truth about why you are keeping it in place, decide to embrace it and stop complaining about it.

14

Most folks are about as happy as they make up their minds to be.

Abraham Lincoln

Decide Now to Be Happy

We often find ourselves in situations that cause us to be unhappy. At least that's what we think - that our unhappiness is due to our situation. We usually think that our situation is beyond our control. The more we ponder our sorry state of affairs, the more we suffer.

One of the surest ways to maintain a life of suffering is to keep your attention on yourself and your problems. This is why therapy is so often ineffective. The therapist working with you usually concentrates your focus on you. Now do not misunderstand. An examination of these areas can indeed be worthwhile if used as the basis from which we make the necessary requests and actions to resolve the issues in question. However, when the sessions remain centered on you and your never-ending personal problems, they serve to keep the very issues you desire to resolve in place. If you want to stop suffering, simply turn your attention off yourself and put it on something outside of you. Take on a new challenge or area of development that will require you to reinvent who you are. Commit to the support or success of another person. Decide to champion another's excellence. Take on a worthwhile cause or challenge and focus on contribution. Doing so will handle your petty concerns. If your life is centered solely on the pursuit of your own happiness, you'll likely never get there.

Suffering involves wanting something you do not have or having something you do not want. If you maintain your focus here without taking any definitive action steps to resolve your dilemma, you keep your unwanted condition in place. Cast off the role of a victim and take full responsibility for your life, relationships and wellbeing.

It's too easy to fall into the trap of thinking that life will be great when some future event happens. It does not matter what the event is. For some it's leaving school, for others going back to school. Some think happiness will come when they get married, others when they get divorced. To some, having kids is the answer. To others, having the kids move out is more like it. The circumstances are irrelevant. Your happiness in any of these scenarios is always in the future. However, as soon as the future arrives, it somehow loses its luster and you are back in the miserable present. You find yourself, once again, living out of your past with your eye on some future event that will make you happy.

Instead of linking your happiness to a future event, decide to be happy by virtue of declaring that you are. Remember, happiness is an interpretation you get to invent or declare as a commitment. When you live your life out of this declaration, you will interpret events from this perspective of being happy instead of them causing you to become unhappy.

Everything that occurs in your life supports you in some way. Believe it and look for verification of that truth. Empowered with this belief, look forward to an exciting, happy life filled with fun and passion.

Creating Happiness

1) Identify any areas of your life that, you feel, cause you to be unhappy. Is your focus on yourself and your own concerns?

2) Declare your decision to be happy. Notice a shift in how you interpret events. Share your decision to be happy with at least five people and request that they remind you of your declaration when they see you straying from it.

3) To what goal, cause, commitment or vision could you shift your focus to make life worth living for the next 150 years?

4) What definitive actions will you take to resolve any stagnant situations in your life?

15

The weak can never forgive.

Forgiveness is the attribute of the strong.

--Mahatma Gandhi

Forgiveness is not an emotion, it's a decision.

--Randall Worley

The Power of Forgiveness

(This chapter was excepted from The Self-Esteem Book: The Ultimate Guide to Boost the Most Underrated Ingredient for Success and Happiness in Life by Dr. Joe Rubino and included here because of the essential nature of this principle for anyone living intentionally.)

There is no more effective way to heal your past and support your relationships to thrive than by forgiving. It is critical that you begin this healing process by forgiving yourself. We are all human and all make mistakes. The tragedy is not in making the mistake but in not having learned from it. And it's never too late to do so.

Part of the challenge is how we relate to mistakes and problems. In our culture, we have determined that challenges of any nature are bad and that we shouldn't make mistakes. With this limiting paradigm, we have very little room to risk, take chances and aggressively pursue our dreams and honor our values. The concern of avoiding mistakes at all cost has us needlessly resign ourselves to a life that is less than ideal. If you can't afford to make a mistake, you won't have the freedom to grow, expand out of your comfort zone and achieve greatness. What if you adopted the perspective that everyone who lives makes mistakes and that the greatest mistake you can make is to have mistakes crush your spirit and steal your fervor for accessing the best that life has to offer? If we view mistakes as an essential component of our evolution, we will see that they actually support us to see things differently. As we continue to learn from them, our awareness increases and we are less likely to repeat these same mistakes.

From this point of view, powerful people focus not on avoiding mistakes but on living their commitments instead. Embrace mistakes, learn from each one and look forward to the insights and gifts that are sure to come from experiencing future mistakes. By shifting our relationship to mistakes and overcoming our fear of making them, we can move on with our lives in a powerful manner. We can expect to make more mistakes, encounter many more challenges and grow from each enriching experience. So, acknowledge yourself for having learned some extremely valuable lessons from your mistakes.

We all do the best we can to not only survive but to actually thrive as we go about our daily lives. We instinctively seek pleasure and avoid pain. Based upon the limited perspective we have as imperfect creatures, we will err from time to time. Please do not misunderstand. I am not condoning hurtful behavior. I am simply suggesting compassion for our human weaknesses. Adopt the attitude that you will continue to make mistakes until the day you draw your last breath. In the grand scheme of things, everything is important and nothing matters so much that we should choose the alternative to risking. This option is the death of our spirit and the resignation that comes with living in fear and playing not to lose instead of to win.

We are often our own harshest critics. When we judge ourselves to be bad and unworthy of love and life's greatest pleasures, we manifest a negative, destructive energy that ensures this be so. Our self-esteem suffers to the extent we maintain our right to punish ourselves for past weaknesses and mistakes. We attract the negative energy we put out into the world. By failing to forgive ourselves, we block the loving energy that cleanses our souls and allows us to share our greatest gift with others, the gift of being the best we can be.

By stubbornly keeping our critical self-judgments and the self-anger that accompanies these in place, we avoid responsibility for making our relationships stronger and our lives work most advantageously. Doing so allows us to shirk liability for communication. We stay angry with ourselves and keep active an unhealthy level of self-pity for our faults. This distracts us from getting on with our lives and cleaning up our mess! It's a lot more difficult to forgive and give up being a victim. Forgiving enables us to proactively get about the business of making our lives and relation ships flourish rather than keep the downward spiral of self-incrimination and blaming others alive. Making mistakes is part of the human condition. It has nothing to do with our worthiness as a person. It also has no bearing on the healthy unconditional self-acceptance essential to high self-esteem.

Taking responsibility for our excellence means committing to no longer act in a manner consistent with past mistakes, but to learn from them instead.

We hate those things about others that we hate most about ourselves. Forgiving ourselves is the first step in clearing the way to forgive others. By forgiving yourself, the toxic resentment that consumes your spirit and destroys self-esteem will give way to the self-love that precedes forgiving and loving others.

Waiting for others to initiate reconciliation will not support your relationships, health or self-image. Healing your troubled past will come from the empathy you get by putting yourself in the other person's world and understanding why he may have acted as he did. By being the first to forgive others, you pave a new road to a future based upon love rather than anger. Remember that anger results from our interpretations about what was done, not the actions themselves.

Forgiving will make you the champion and designer of your future self, a self you can feel good about.

Likewise, there may be some people who you have wronged. Look to see if there is anything you can do to make amends for hurting them with past behavior. Clean up misspoken words and acknowledge mistakes. Acknowledge the casual promises that you blew off as being unimportant. Offer a sincere apology if you have erred and commit to make things right and repair the damaged relationship, if possible. Your reparation should be appropriate for the damage you caused and directed at the person harmed. When you actively accept responsibility for your part in failed communication or a wounded relationship, you act with the courage to make things right. This commitment blazes a trail to a new way of being.

When you apologize for past mistakes and take appropriate action to clean up the mess created, you take responsibility for your part by giving a 100 percent effort toward healing the relationship. However the other person chooses to respond, take comfort in knowing you have done whatever you could to repair the harm. It will support you to be committed to healing the relationship without an attachment to having the other person respond in kind. By showing a willingness to repair the situation to the best of your ability, you have done your part to initiate a healing of the relationship. Keep the door open to communication, congratulate yourself for courageously taking action in the direction of completion and get on with your life. When you have done everything you can to right a past indiscretion, it will not support you to continue to berate yourself about what was done. We all make mistakes. All we can ask of ourselves is to continue to learn from our actions, commit to honoring others and take responsibility for being the person we declare ourselves to be. Again, this does not excuse hurtful or wrongful action. It simply means acting from love upon realizing you have caused another pain or loss.

With this foundation of love, you are now free to declare who you are to the world rather than have resentment dictate your reactions. The attachment to making yourself and others wrong will fade and a commitment to deliberately designing the person you are will be possible. Miracles will manifest and your self-image and personal power will soar.

Practicing Forgiveness

List all the items for which you have not yet forgiven yourself and others. Create a plan to clean up any misspoken words, acknowledge mistakes and apologize for any errors you may have made. For those deceased or those you cannot or choose not to achieve completion with in person, write a letter expressing your thoughts, emotions and forgiveness. Mailing the letter is optional.

16

No explanation ever explains the necessity of making one.

Elbert Hubbard,
American author and editor

Giving Away Your Power - Because

We are addicted to needing a justification for everything we do. We look for a reason to accompany every event. This logic causes us to give away our power to whatever external events come our way. No one can make you sad, angry or scared. No one can make you do anything. To believe that they can is to give away the power that is rightfully yours.

Whenever we justify what we do, we lose our ability to act independently of circumstances. To say that you did anything because of something else is not only untrue, but it makes you dependent on external forces. You give up your autonomy in an attempt to come up with an explanation. This mode of thinking is so deeply ingrained in our culture that we have trained ourselves to expect an explanation or a "because" for all our behavior.

Whenever we explain our behavior away as the result of something that happened outside our will, we are guilty of confusing the facts with our interpretation of the particulars. This is always a lie to some degree. As an example, you might say, "I'm late for work because my car broke down." We are thoroughly conditioned to buy into a statement like this, taking it as the truth. But what if you were told that you had won $10 million and the money was yours as long as you arrived on time to claim it by Monday morning at 9 A.M.? With so much riding on your punctuality, perhaps you might arrive a day early just so you don't miss out! The point is, you were not late because of any reason outside your control. You simply did not take total responsibility for arriving on time. When we commit to something and don't do it, perhaps it may not have been quite important enough for us to keep our commitment.

If you begin to closely examine every time you or others use "because" as a justification, you'll start to see there is always a story involved that is subject to interpretation.

The man beats his wife because his father beat him when he was a child. Is this true or is it a justification to absolve the man of responsibility for his actions?

You give your power away when you assign responsibility to some outside force. You see, the man in the above example who beat his wife was himself beaten as a child because his father beat him as well. But his father did so because he could not deal with his alcoholic wife. And she drank because her mother never loved her as a child.

Whenever you confuse the facts with your interpretations, you give your power away in the process. You always have the ability to create an empowering interpretation that supports you in moving a situation forward.

It will involve giving up your desire to be right about something in favor of opting to have life work for all involved.

Being Responsible for All Your Actions

1) Notice whenever you use "because" as a justification for doing or not doing something. Note these occasions in your journal.

2) Take full responsibility for every aspect of your life. Record in your journal those instances when you notice that you're not. Record the action steps you will take for all areas of life that arc not up to your standards.

17

Become a possibilitarian. No matter how dark things seem to be or actually are, raise your sights and see possibilities - always see them for they're always there.

Norman Vincent Peale,
American clergyman and
advocate of the power of positive thinking

Living in an Either/Or World

Most of us have been conditioned since birth to see the world from an either/or perspective. Either you are right or you are wrong. Either you are winning or I am. Either you get your way or I get mine. This living in either/or separates us from others. We avoid mutuality in favor of either focusing on ourselves or on what's going on with the other person. The inevitable result is the creation of a problem.

For a problem to exist, there must be an equal and opposite force involved.

----------------------- ⬣ -----------------------

If the forces are not equal, one party will dominate and there will not be a problem. Think of a 350-pound football lineman facing off against a 125-pound opponent. There is no contest. The bigger one will have his way every time. If the forces are not opposing ones, there will also be no conflicting result.

------------------- ➡
⬅-----------------

Like two ships passing in the night, no problem will ensue.

However, when the forces are both opposing and equal, a problem or impasse will result.

The resolution to the problem or stalemate will come as a result of shifting from either/or to and/both. By doing so, your relationship to the problem changes. You go from looking to dominate to searching for mutuality, win-win as opposed to win-lose.

This is what responsibility is all about. Responsibility is an and/both conversation.

It's a meeting in the middle, a dance of energies between two people. Being responsible means considering what is going on with the other person. When you understand that responsibility means you are the source of everything that shows up in life, your life will be altered forever.

The concept that you are responsible for everything occurring in your life isn't necessarily true. It's simply a conceptual tool, a stand you take to shift responsibility from the other person or circumstances to you, elevating your level of personal power.

Let's look at what being responsible when making tough choices really means. For example, do you devote your energies to your job or to your family? Do you get your way or give in to the other guy? Do you go back to school or do you get a job? Do you stay home with the kids or go off to work? Do you save for college expenses or do you live for today?

We are so accustomed to living in either/or that we often do not think of looking at how we might make it an and/both or win/win conversation. Responsibility means looking for how it can work out for you, the other person and for life in general. Training yourself to begin to look at every impasse you encounter from the perspective of and/both responsibility, always keeping open to possibilities, will have a dramatic impact on your life.

Shifting From Either/Or to And/Both

1) Begin to notice when you find yourself confronted with an either/or or win/lose choice. Look instead to responsibly shift your perspective to and/both and win/win.

2) What is it costing you in terms of your relationships and the creation of possibilities by staying in either/or thinking?

3) Claim responsibility by creating an and/both, win/win scenario where you are currently in an either/or or win/lose situation.

- At home
- At work
- With friends

18

Being a hero is about the shortest-lived profession on earth.

Will Rogers,
American humorist, actor and author

Putting Others on a Pedestal

Are you in the habit of putting the people you respect on a pedestal? Do you idolize what they say and believe that they can do no wrong? Be careful. As surely as you put them on the pedestal, they will fall from their lofty perch. Putting others on a pedestal allows you to avoid responsibility for getting what you need from the relationship. By placing blind trust in what they say, you set yourself up for disappointment when things do not turn out as planned. Because you hold the individual in such high esteem, they inevitably will disappoint you when they fail to live up to the unrealistic expectations you have placed upon them. This behavior is a setup to avoid responsibility if you believe that if things did not work out, it would not be your fault. You have it set up such that you trust them completely and it will be their fault if they let you down and betray that trust.

Consider the following approach. Instead of putting someone on a pedestal, create the space for him or her to interact powerfully with you. By granting this space, you empower the person you respect to offer coaching and feedback. You can then objectively evaluate how this feedback might affect you. Consider what is offered not as "the truth" but as a possibility that you evaluate to see if it might support you. Remember that no one is infallible. People can and will make mistakes and be misguided in their thoughts and deeds at times. By providing another the space to contribute to you, you give up your right to shoot them down off their pedestal when they do not meet your expectations.

Creating Space for Others
to Contribute to You

1) Who have you put up on a pedestal?

2) Shift your relationship with them by creating the space for them to contribute to you without their needing to be infallible.

3) Describe in your journal how you will go about doing this.

19

Who brings a tale takes two away.

Irish proverb

Putting an End to Gossip

By definition, gossip is any conversation about a third party that takes place in that person's absence and that has the characteristic of undermining their reputation, stature or well-being. Gossip is equivalent to cancer in the realm of communication. If left unchecked, it can spread quickly, putting an end to healthy productive relationships. People that gossip freely to you about others will likely gossip about you when given the opportunity.

Fortunately, there is an effective means to stop gossip dead in its tracks. When you are in the presence of someone who is damaging the reputation of another through gossip, simply say, "I am concerned to hear you say that about Jane, and I know that she would be as well. So, let's get her on the phone right now so that we might clear this up once and for all."

When people realize that you refuse to be a co-conspirator in their gossiping, they will cease to gossip in your presence. The result will be a healthier relationship for all concerned and a respect for your unwillingness to join in behavior that undermines another.

Putting an End to Gossip

1) Where have you been party to undermining the reputation of another through gossip? How often does this happen? Note the situations in your journal.

2) What actions will you take to put an end to this behavior on your part and to clean up any damage you may have done?

3) How will you discourage others from including you in gossip?

20

Human beings are perhaps never more frightening than when they are convinced beyond doubt that they are right.

Laurens Van Der Post,
English author and poet

What you are afraid of overtakes you.

Estonian proverb

Life's challenges are not supposed to paralyze you, they're supposed to help you discover who you are.

Bernice Johnson Reagon,
American Historian, born 1942

Becoming a Perpetual Student and Allowing Difficult People and Challenging Situations to Be Your Teacher

While the vast majority of people view the daily challenges that life throws across our paths as inconvenient at best and a real nuisance that we should attempt to avoid at nearly all costs at worst, there is another possible perspective we might adopt to maximize our personal power. Rather than avoid these unpleasant and disruptive challenges, we can instead embrace them as an opportunity to learn something about ourselves and our ability to deal effectively with the trials they pose.

When things do not go our way, rather than blame someone or become resigned to seeing the circumstances as yet more evidence demonstrating our bad luck or deficiency in character, we might instead look for ways that we can learn and grow from the experience. If we take on the perspective that each challenge is sent our way with a gift of wisdom attached to it, we can transform how we see and respond to each episode. How we react to difficult situations will depend upon how we see our role in having brought them about. We can decide to be a victim, at the mercy of each difficulty or we can look for what part we may have played to contribute to it in some way.

Now, I am not suggesting that we blame ourselves or find fault with our performance as those lacking high self-esteem might be prone to do. Instead, I am proposing that we look at the stressful situation to see if we might have handled it differently had we realized some insight we now were able to glean by studying the event. By looking for possible contributory factors that resulted in having the situation turn out as it did, we can learn from our inquiry and act differently in the future.

This possibility to impact our experience is particularly rich when it comes to interacting with difficult people. We can shun the people we hold as having little or nothing of value to teach us, or we can hold them as a precious resource being sent our way to support our personal development. The more difficult the personalities, the more effective we will need to become in dealing powerfully with them and the more we have the potential to learn about ourselves and our ability to impact a result.

The key to interacting effectively with those we consider to be challenging people is to create the space for them to be the unique, imperfect individuals that they are. This means accepting their quirky behavior, at times difficult interpretations, irritating habits, and less than effective communication skills. Rather than hoping to change them, reprimand them, or try to fix them, it is more productive to accept what you might consider to be their faults and allow them the ability to be who they are. When you cease to oppose who they are, they will, in turn, no longer have to defend themselves or try to avoid being dominated by you. They will be less likely to find fault with you and less likely to need to exert control over you. With the generous allowance you've created for their humanity, you can now look at how you might be most effective in influencing them so that life works for both of you.

As we've discussed before, the secret to effectively interacting with people who would normally present us with a challenge is to manage our emotional state. Rather than react to what they say and do and thereby give away our personal power, we have the ability to monitor what would have been our typical emotional responses and act intentionally instead, without the driving emotion of anger, sadness, fear, or any other negative force that breeds upset and makes effectual communication unlikely.

When we give up our need to dominate a situation, control the other person, or be right about something, we gain the ability to interact powerfully and without a damaging reaction fuelled by negative emotions.

Allowing Difficult People and Challenging Situations to Be Your Teacher

1) As you go about your day, identify each challenging event to reflect upon how you might deal with the situation most effectively.

2) Practice allowing others to have the space to be who they are, complete with all their faults and shortcomings, and without the need to change or fix them. How does doing so influence your relationship with someone you would consider to be a difficult person?

3) For each problematic situation you find yourself in, record in your journal how you may have contributed to the difficulty by your action or inaction. What could you do differently next time?

21

The important thing is this: To be able at any moment to sacrifice what we are for what we could become.

Charles Debois,
American author

It's Never Handled

Now that you have read this far and hopefully taken the necessary time to experience the various principles presented, it's time to reinforce a few important points.

First, personal development is a never-ending, lifelong process. There is no arriving, only experiencing. I suggest that you go back to the beginning of this book (and to the beginning of Book I as well) and re-read each principle with the intention of identifying those that would most impact your life, happiness and personal effectiveness if you were to seriously develop them. For some, acquiring the necessary principles and skills may take additional weeks or months. Others will require a far greater effort. Make a commitment to keep up some consistent level of activity to expand who you are each day of your life, bringing you closer to realizing your full potential. No matter what the area of your development, immerse yourself in the question and stay there for as long as it takes to expand your perspective and experience the breakthroughs that await your discovery. And by all means, enjoy the process and have fun.

Self-discovery and personal development can only open the door for you to begin to uncover what is next for you in life. For meaningful transformation to take place, information must lead to a commitment to action and the willingness to put yourself - and who you think you are - at risk.

Breakthroughs in your understanding and your effectiveness with others will result from your courage to reinvent who you are minute by minute as you develop more and more of the principles that will increase your personal power. Make the most of what life hands you, committing yourself to the actions that support who you choose to be in the world, but not becoming attached to the results.

Lastly, decide to live the rest of your life out of your vision. Your vision for yourself and your family. Your vision for the world and for humanity. Your vision for what is possible to accomplish when you act out of your commitment to excellence, love and all of the ideals you hold dear. Don't let your life go by without championing your own magnificence and that of others. Too often, we play small, not fully realizing what we are capable of accomplishing. Decide now to go for the brass ring with a commitment to kill the resignation that has you settle for anything less than all that you can be.

Develop clarity around what would be worth playing for if you lived another 300 years. What could you take on to have every morning of every day filled with a passion that would have your spirit soar into action? Let this passion fuel your days as you pursue a life vision that would impact both you and others.

Become very clear about what it is costing you not to play full out at life. What is it costing you in terms of possibilities for your life, happiness, vitality and contribution to the world? When you are totally in touch with the costs of playing small, you will realize that your only real choice is to live out of your commitment to be the best you can be, always in pursuit of making the most of your personal power.

As George Bernard Shaw said. "This is the true joy in life, being used for a purpose recognized by yourself as a mighty one; the being a force of nature instead of a feverish, selfish little clod of ailments and grievances complaining that the world will not devote itself to making you happy. I am of the opinion that my life belongs to the whole community and as long as I live, it is my privilege to do for it whatever I can. I want to be thoroughly used up when I die, for the harder I work, the more I live. I rejoice in life for it's own sake. Life is no 'brief candle' to me. It is a sort of splendid torch which I have got hold of for the moment, and I want to make it burn as brightly as possible before handing it on to future generations."

Do not let the principles presented in this book live only as sterile information, useless without your commitment to applying them in your own life. Ask yourself constantly:

What are the possibilities for your life?

What will you do to make the most of them?

What is next for you?

Dr. Joe Rubino is widely acknowledged as one of North America's foremost success and productivity coaches. He is the CEO of The Center for Personal Reinvention. To date more than 1 million people have benefited from his coaching and leadership development training. In partnership with co-founder, Dr. Tom Ventullo, the Center provides coaching, productivity and leadership development courses that champion people to maximize their personal power and effectiveness.

He is the author of 9 best-selling books and 2 audio programs available worldwide in 19 languages. These include:
• The Magic Lantern: A Fable about Leadership, Personal Excellence, and Empowerment

- The Legend of the Light-Bearers: A Fable about Personal Reinvention and Global Transformation
- The Self-Esteem Book: The Ultimate Guide to Boost the Most Underrated Ingredient for Success and Happiness in Life
- Secrets of Building a Million Dollar Network Marketing Organization from a Guy Who's Been There, Done That and Shows You How You Can Do It Too
- The 7-Step System to Building a $1,000,000 Network Marketing Organization: How to Achieve Financial Freedom through Network Marketing
- The Ultimate Guide to Network Marketing
- 10 Weeks to Network Marketing Success - CD or Cassette Album plus Workbook
- Secret #1 - Self-Motivation Audible and Subliminal Affirmation CDs
- 15 Secrets Every Network Marketer Must Know

• The Success Code: 29 Principles for Achieving Maximum Abundance, Success, Charisma, and Personal Power in Your Life
• The Success Code, Book II: More Authentic Power Principles for Creating Your Dream Life

To request information about any of The Center for Personal Reinvention's programs or to order any of Dr. Rubino's books, visit http://www.CenterForPersonalReinvention.com

Recommended Personal Development Programs

The Center for Personal Reinvention
Dr. Joe Rubino and Dr. Tom Ventullo

Where are you stopped in your life and in your business?

Where is there an unacceptable level of resignation or conflict?

Where are there interpersonal listening and communications skills lacking?

Where is there a missing in terms of partnership, commitment and vision?

The world we live and work in is marked by unprecedented change and fraught with new and complex challenges. For many of us, life begins to look like an uphill struggle to survive instead of a fun and exciting opportunity to grow, risk, and play full out in partnership with others. The stresses, conflicts and frustrations we experience daily need not be so.

In place of these, there exists another possibility.

...To live and work in choice - empowered by the challenges of life.

...To champion others to achieve excellence in a nurturing environment that fosters partnerships.

...To acquire the success distinctions that support mutuality, creativity and harmony.

...To take on the art of listening and communicating in such a way that others are impacted to see new possibilities for accomplishment, partnership and excellence.

Reinventing ourselves, our relationships and our perception of the world is the result of a never ending commitment to our own personal magnificence and to that of others. It is made possible through the acquisition of approximately 50 key distinctions that cause people to begin to view life and people in an entirely different way. When people really get these distinctions, life, relationships, and new possibilities for breakthroughs show up in a totally different way. Through the use of cutting edge concepts as a vibrant basis for learning, growing and acting, The Center For Personal Reinvention is successful in shifting how life shows up for people by supporting them to self-discover these life-changing foundational principles.

With this program, YOU will:

•Uncover the secrets to accessing your personal power while maximizing your productivity.

•Gain clarity on exactly what it will take to reach your goals with velocity.

• Create a structure for skyrocketing your effectiveness while developing new and empowering partnerships.

• Learn how taking total responsibility for every aspect of your life and business can result in breakthrough performance.

• Discover what the key elements are to a detailed action plan and how to reach your goals in record time.

•Acquire the keys to listening and communicating effectively and intentionally

•Recognize and shift out of self-defeating thoughts and actions.

•Gain the insight to better understand others with new compassion and clarity

•Learn how to develop the charisma necessary to attract others to you.

•Experience the confidence and inner peace that comes from stepping into leadership.

The Center for Personal Reinvention

...Bringing people and companies back to life!

Customized Courses and Programs Personally Designed For Achieving Maximum Results

Areas of Focus include:

Designing Your Future

Making Life and Businesses Work

Generating Infinite Possibilities

Creating Conversations for Mutuality

Commitment Management

Personal Coaching and Development

Maximizing Personal Effectiveness

Breakthrough Productivity

Leadership Development

Relationship and Team Building

Conflict Resolution

Listening for Solutions

Systems for Personal Empowerment

Personal and Productivity Transformation

Designing Structures for Accomplishment

Creating Empowered Listening Attitudes

Possibility Thinking

Accelerating Action in a Forward
Direction

Structures for Team Accountability

Innovative Thinking

Completing With the Past

Creating a Life of No Regrets

The Center for Personal Reinvention champions companies and individuals to achieve their potential through customized programs addressing specific needs consistent with their vision for the future.

Contact us today to explore
how we might impact your world!

The Center For Personal Reinvention
PO Box 217, Boxford, MA 01921

drjrubino@email.com
Fax: (630) 982-2134

Books by Dr. Joe Rubino

The Self-Esteem Book: The Ultimate Guide to Boost the Most Underrated Ingredient for Success and Happiness in Life

With this book YOU will:

· Uncover the source of your lack of self-esteem

· Heal the past and stop the downward spiral of self-sabotage

· Replace negative messages with new core beliefs that support your happiness and excellence

· Realize the secret to reclaiming your personal power

· See how you can be strong and authentic. Use your vulnerability as a source of power

· Design a new self-image that supports your magnificence

· Realize the power of forgiveness

· Discover the secret to un upset-free life

· Re-establish your worth and reinvent yourself to be your best
· Create a vision of a life of no regrets

To order your Ultimate Self-Esteem Pack including The Self-Esteem Book, visit Http://www.TheSelfEsteemBook.com

THE 7-Step Success System to Building a Million Dollar Network marketing Dynasty: How to Achieve Financial Independence through Network Marketing

This book is perhaps the most comprehensive step-by-step guide ever written on how to build a lasting, multi-million dollar organization. Success Magazine called Master Instructor, Dr. Joe Rubino a Millionaire Maker in their landmark "We Create Millionaires" cover story because of his ability to pass along the power to achieve top-level success to others. Now you can learn exactly how Dr.

Joe built his own dynasty so that you can too. Follow the 7 detailed steps-to-success blueprint and join the ranks of network marketing's top income earners.

Step 1: Visioning - Establish Your Reasons for Joining & Create a Compelling Vision

Step 2: Planning - Create a Master Plan That Will Support You to Realize Your Vision

Step 3: Prospecting - Effective Prospecting: Who, Where, and How and How Many?

Step 4: Enrolling - The Power to Enroll: How to Become an Enrollment Machine

Step 5: Training - Train like a Master Instructor: Structures for Successful Partnerships

Step 6: Personal Development - Grow as Fast as Your Organization Does: Create Structures for Personal Excellence

Step 7: Stepping Into Leadership - The Keys to Developing Other Self-Motivated Leaders

The Ultimate Guide to Network Marketing: 37 Top Network marketing Income-Earners Share Their Most Preciously-Guarded Secrets to Building Extreme Wealth

In The Ultimate Guide to Network marketing, Dr. Joe Rubino presents a wide variety of proven business-building techniques and tactics taken from thirty-seven of the most successful network marketers and trainers in the industry. Together, these thirty-seven experts present a comprehensive resource for the specialized information and strategies that network marketers need to grow their businesses and achieve top-level success.

The three primary elements of successful network marketing are prospecting, following up, and enrolling. Here, you'll find a unique blend of expert opinion and practical advice on how to be more successful at these vital tasks. This invaluable resource lets you explore the many various effective tactics and techniques the contributors used to make their fortunes-so you can pick what works best for you.

Inside, you'll find unbeatable advice on these topics and many more:

• Crafting a winning attitude that attracts others
• Mastering the art of persuasion
• Instant changes that make you more believable when speaking
• Identifying a prospect's most important values
• Simple, valuable skills you should teach your team
• Tactics for convincing skeptical and reluctant prospects
• How to work the "cold" market for prospects
• Seven profitable Internet prospecting tools
• Prospecting at home parties, trade shows, and fairs

- Direct mail prospecting tips
- How to become a great leader

Revealing a world of secrets it would take a lifetime in the industry to amass, The Ultimate Guide to Network marketing is a one-of-a-kind resource that will put you on the inside track to success. Loaded with hard-earned wisdom and essential techniques, it will advise your every step as you build your network marketing business.

Secrets Of Building A Million Dollar Network marketing Organization From A Guy Who's Been There Done That And Shows You How To Do It Too.

Learn the Keys to Success in Building Your Network-Marketing Business.

With This Book You Will:

•Get the 6 keys that unlock the door to success in network marketing.

•Learn how to build your business free from doubt and fear.

•Discover how the way you listen has limited your success. And ...

•Accomplish your goals in record time by shifting your listening.

•Use the Zen of Prospecting to draw people to you like a magnet.

•Build rapport and find your prospect's hot buttons instantly.

•Pick the perfect prospecting approach for you.

•Turn any prospect's objection into the very reason they join.

•Identify your most productive prospecting sources. And ...

•Win the numbers game of network marketing.

•Develop a step-by-step business plan that ensures your future.

•Design a Single Daily Action that increases your income 10 times.

•Rate yourself as a top sponsor and business partner.

•Create a passionate vision that guarantees your success.

And More!!!

10 Weeks to Network-Marketing Success: The Secrets to Launching Your Very Own Million-Dollar Organization in a 10-Week Business-Building and Personal-Development Self-Study Course

Learn the business-building and personal-development secrets that will put you squarely on the path to network-marketing success. 10 Weeks to Network-Marketing Success is a powerful course that will grow your business with velocity and change your life!

With this course, YOU will:

• Learn exactly how to set up a powerful 10-week action plan that will propel your business growth.

• Learn how to prospect in your most productive niche markets.

• Discover your most effective pathways to success.

- Learn how to persuasively influence your prospects by listening to contribute value.
- Build your business rapidly by making powerful requests.
- Discover the secret to acting from your commitments.
- Create a powerful life-changing structure for personal development.
- See the growth that comes from evaluating your progress on a regular basis.
- Learn how listening in a new and powerful way will skyrocket your business.
- Uncover the secret to accepting complete responsibility for your business.
- Learn how to transform problems into breakthroughs.
- Develop the charisma that allows you to instantly connect with others on a heart-to-heart level.
- Identify the secrets to stepping into leadership and being the source of your success.
- And much more!

The Success Code

The 10 Weeks to Network-Marketing Success Program contains 10 weekly exercises on 4 CDs or 6 Cassettes plus a 37-page workbook.

The Success Code: 29 Principles for Achieving Maximum Abundance, Success, Charisma, and Personal Power in Your Life

What exactly distinguishes those who are effective in their relationships, productive in business and happy, powerful, and successful in their approach to life from those who struggle, suffer, and fail? That is the key question that *The Success Code* explores in life-changing detail. The information, examples, experiences, and detailed exercises offered will produce life-altering insights for readers who examine who they are being on a moment-to-moment basis that either contributes to increasing their personal effectiveness, happiness and power - or not. As you commit to an inquiry around what it takes to access your personal power, you will gain the tools to overcome any challenges or limiting thoughts and behavior and discover exactly what it means to be the best you can be.

With this book YOU will:

• Uncover the secrets to accessing your personal power.

• Create a structure for maximizing your effectiveness with others.

• Learn to take total responsibility for everything in your life.

• Discover the key elements to accomplishment and how to reach your goals in record time.

• Identify your life rules and discover how honoring your core values can help you maximize productivity.

• Complete your past and design your future on purpose.

• Discover the keys to communicating effectively and intentionally.

• Stop complaining and start doing.

• Seize your personal power and conquer resignation in your life.

• Learn how to generate conversations that uncover new possibilities.

• See how embracing problems can lead to positive breakthroughs in life.

• Leave others whole while realizing the power of telling the truth.

• Learn how to develop the charisma necessary to attract others to you

The Success Code, Book II: More Authentic Power Principles for Creating Your Dream Life

This revealing book continues where *The Success Code, Book I* left off with more powerful insights into what it takes to be most happy, successful and effective with others.

With this book YOU will:

• Discover the keys to unlock the door to success and happiness.

• Learn how your listening determines what you attract to you.

• And how to shift your listening to access your personal power.

• See how creating a clear intention can cause miracles to show up around you.

• Learn the secrets to making powerful requests to get what you want from others.

• Discover how to fully connect with and champion others to realize their greatness.

• Learn to create interpretations that support your excellence and avoid those that keep you small.

• Develop the power to speak and act from your commitments.

• See how communication with others can eliminate unwanted conditions from your life.

• Discover the secret to being happy and eliminating daily upsets.

• Learn how to put an end to gossip and stop giving away your power.

• Develop the ability to lead your life with direction and purpose and discover what it's costing you not to do so.
• And More!!

Dr. Joe Rubino's personal development book series is a powerful course in becoming the person you wish to be. Read these books, take on the success principles discussed and watch your life and business transform and flourish.

The Magic Lantern:
A Fable about Leadership, Personal Excellence and Empowerment

Set in the magical world of Center Earth, inhabited by dwarves, elves, goblins, and wizards, The Magic Lantern is a tale of personal development that teaches the keys to success and happiness. This fable examines what it means to take on true leadership while learning to become maximally effective with everyone we meet.

Renowned personal development trainer, coach, and veteran author, Dr. Joe Rubino tells the story of a group of dwarves and their young leader who go off in search of the secrets to a life that works, a life filled with harmony and endless possibilities and void of the regrets and upsets that characterize most people's existence. With a mission to restore peace and harmony to their village in turmoil, the characters overcome the many challenges they encounter along their eventful journey. Through self-discovery, they develop the principles necessary to be the best that they can be as they step into leadership and lives of contribution to others.

The Magic Lantern teaches us:

• the power of forgiveness

• the meaning of responsibility and commitment

• what leadership is really all about

• the magic of belief and positive expectation

• the value of listening as an art

• the secret to mastering one's emotions and actions

• and much more.

It combines the spellbinding storytelling reminiscent of Tolkien's *The Hobbit* with the personal development tools of the great masters.

The Legend of the Light-Bearers: A Fable about Personal Reinvention and Global Transformation

Is it ever too late for a person to take on personal reinvention and transform his or her life? Can our planet right itself and reverse centuries of struggle, hatred and warfare? Are love, peace, and harmony achievable possibilities for the world's people? *The Legend of the Light-Bearers* is a tale about vision, courage, and commitment, set in the magical world of Center Earth. In this much anticipated prequel to Dr. Joe Rubino's internationally best-selling book, *The Magic Lantern: A Fable about Leadership, Personal Excellence and Empowerment*, the process of

personal and global transformation is
explored within the guise of an enchanting
fable. As the action unfolds in the world following the great Earth Changes, this personal
development parable explores the nature of
hatred and resignation, the secrets to transformation, and the power of anger and the
means to overcoming it and replacing it with
love. It shows what can happen when people
live values-based lives and are guided by
their life purposes instead of their destructive
moods and their need to dominate others. If
ever our world needed a roadmap to peace
and cooperation and our people, a guide to
personal empowerment and happiness, they
do now...and this is the book.

15 Secrets Every Network Marketer Must Know: Essential Elements and Skills Required to Achieve 6 & 7 Figure Success in Network Marketing

Each year in North America, more than 13
million people participate in network market-

ing, selling tens of billions of dollars of goods and services. The top moneymakers in the business take home six- or seven-figures. Wouldn't you love to know how they do it? With *15 Secrets Every Network Marketer Must Know*, you will!

Written by top expert marketers Dr. Joe Rubino and John Terhune, this practical, one-of-a-kind guide explains fifteen key network marketing principles-the core secrets to unlimited success. The principles, strategies, and tactics presented in this book will help you maximize your personal effectiveness, attitude, and behavior as you build your dynasty on a solid foundation that will ensure it will last long into the future. Based on proven, time-tested strategies and the long experience of two well-known and extremely well-qualified authors, this book is an indispensable tool for every network marketer, even those just starting out.

15 Secrets Every Network Marketer Must Know will put you on the path to real wealth with step-by-step guidance on:

- Getting yourself into a successful frame of mind
- Using failure as an advantage
- Mastering self-discipline and redirecting the urge to quit to your advantage
- Developing long-term goals that drive your daily activities
- Building and finessing a great, money-making list
- Developing great leaders and associates
- Following up effectively
- And much more

SECRET #1 - SELF MOTIVATION

Utilize The Latest in *Whole Brain Inner Talk*™ Technology to take a trip to a deeper dimension of power within yourself and tap into The Most Important Secret To Success In Network Marketing...**SELF-MOTIVATION!**

Thought Modification
Made Easy Audio CD Series

Put to work for you the powerful combination of the latest in patented and scientifically proven audible and subliminal brain wave technology developed by Dr. Eldon Taylor, the world's foremost expert on offsetting negative information by inputting positive messages directly into the subconscious. This safe and highly effective proven technology has been independently researched at leading institutions such as Stanford University. For the first time ever, this technology has been combined with the 124 thought altering positive self talk affirmations developed by Dr. Joe Rubino, one of North America's foremost business trainers and coaches- the man Success Magazine called a "Millionaire Maker". The result is a remarkable audio series that will give you the power to alter any limiting thoughts...The power to maximize your personal effectiveness to rapidly build your MLM business on purpose and with confidence.

This revolutionary two CD set consists of one Positive Self-Talk Program, which combines audible affirmations with the shadowed subliminal Inner Talk® affirmations, and one Ozo self motivation program. Use the first tape at least once a day playing it in the background in your car or while you work or play. Use the second tape with headphones when you can take 20 minutes and close your eyes. The special frequencies will entrain brain wave activity and produce an optimal state for learning and conditioning new patterns, energizing you into action and filling your being with total confidence.

Listen to Secret #1 - Self-Motivation before you prospect and you'll feel 10 feet tall and bullet proof! It's like hiring Dr. Joe Rubino as your personal success coach!

Vision Works Publishing
PO Box 217
Boxford, MA 01921

To Order any of Dr. Joe Rubino's Life-
Impacting Books or Audio Programs, Visit
http://www.CenterForPersonalReinvention.com

Call (888) 821-3135
Fax: (630) 982-2134
Email: VisionWorksBooks@Email.com

QUANTITY DISCOUNTS AVAILABLE